Wonderful Wife™

A JOURNAL FOR THE HEART OF
A WONDERFUL WIFE™

DAVID AND AMANDA REIGLE

FEELS LIKE FUN ® PUBLICATIONS

For more information, please address Feels Like Fun ® Publications Subsidiary Rights Department, PO BOX 14206 Palm Desert, CA 92260. First Feels Like Fun ® LLC First Edition Paperback June 2022. Shoulder Panda ™ "bear image" and all assets whereof, are trademarks of the Feels Like Fun ® Publications program. Feels Like Fun ® Publications' serve Feels Like Fun® LLC and their clients.

For more information, please contact us at branding@feelslikefun.com Interior design by David and Amanda Reigle ISBN Feels Like Fun® Publications, 2022

Respect, Love, Joy,
Peace, Longsuffering,
Kindness, Goodness,
Faithfulness, Gentleness
& Self-control to the

wives and to the husbands.

Abundant

DEAR HUSBAND,

I AM IN LOVE WITH YOU. I AM
SATISFIED IN THIS LIFE WITH
YOU.

YOU AND I ARE UNDER GRACE, IN
THE MOST PERFECT WAY.

 ♡ YOUR WIFE

1. Appreciation

2. Consideration

3. Love

EVERYTHING IS
WORKING OUT.

DEAR
HUSBAND,

YOU ARE
BRILLIANT.

♡ YOUR
WIFE

1. ....
2. ....
3. ....

1. ....
2. ....
3. ....

MY LOVE,

THANK YOU FOR BEING MY BEST
FRIEND.

THANK YOU FOR ENCOURAGING
MY INTERESTS.

♡ YOUR WIFE

1.

Appreciation

2.

Consideration

3.

Joy

grateful _____ Date: _____

_____
_____
_____

grateful _____ Date: _____

_____
_____
_____

grateful _____ Date: _____

_____
_____
_____

Checking in

MY NEW IDEA

TO MY
HUSBAND,

I LOVE YOUR
COMPANY

I LOVE
THINKING
ABOUT GOING
ON
ADVENTURES
WITH YOU.

♡ YOUR WIFE

CHARACTER

☆ ☆ ☆ ☆ ☆

1. Appreciation

2. Consideration

3. Peace

MY LOVE,

THANK YOU FOR
YOUR KINDNESS.

THANK YOU FOR
KISSING ME AND
HOLDING ME IN
FRONT OF YOUR
FAMILY.

♡ YOUR WIFE

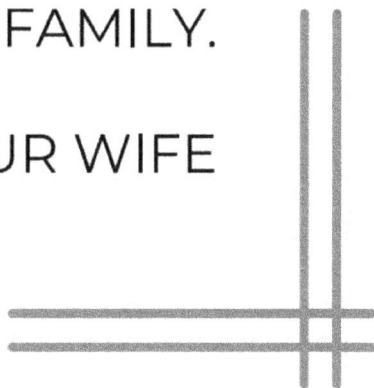

GET TO
KNOW THY SELF

○ _____

○ _____

○ _____

○ _____

○

DEAR
HUSBAND,

I LOVE THAT I
DON'T HAVE TO
BE WITHOUT
YOUR HUGS
AND KISSES
AND HIGH
FIVES.

♡ YOUR WIFE

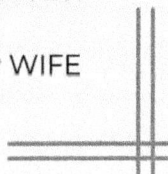

My Husband is:

TO MY
HUSBAND,

THIS IS A NOTE
TO YOU.

I TRUST YOU
AND I ♡ U.

♡ YOUR WIFE

1. Appreciation

2. Consideration

3. Patience (Longsuffering)

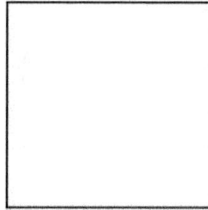

DEAR HUSBAND,

BEING YOUR WIFE IS AN HONOR.

MAY YOUR PEACE AND PATIENCE
CONTINUE TO BE A GUIDING LIGHT IN THIS
WORLD.

♡ YOUR WIFE

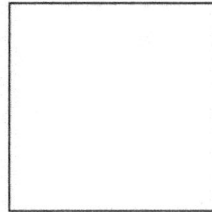
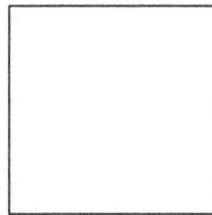

DEAR HUSBAND,

I LOVE AND APPRECIATE EVERYTHING
THAT YOU DO TO CARE FOR ME AND
THIS FAMILY. I LOVE THINKING ABOUT
YOU HAVING A GREAT DAY!

♡ YOUR WIFE

Planning

○

○

○

DEAR HUSBAND,

YOU ARE THE
MOST
WONDERFUL MAN
THAT I HAVE EVER
KNOWN.

YOU ARE A
TREASURE.

♡ YOUR WIFE

I LIKE THINKING
ABOUT
_____

○

○

○

ACCOMPLISHED

DEAR
HUSBAND,

MAY WE
CONTINUE
TO SEEK
DIVINE
GUIDANCE
TOGETHER.

♡ YOUR
WIFE

☆ ☆ ☆ ☆ ☆

THINGS WE LIKE

THINGS THAT MAKE OUR BODIES HAPPY

WHAT'S GOOD

HELLO MY
LOVE,

YOU ARE SO
PRECIOUS.

I APPRECIATE
THAT YOU
CHOSE ME.

♡ YOUR WIFE

DATE

DARLING, WHEN NOTHING ELSE MAKES SENSE, YOU DO. ♡ YOUR WIFE

1. Appreciation

2. Consideration

3. Kindness

What is happening

- ♡ _____
- ♡ _____
- ♡ _____

MY HUSBAND,

MAY YOUR HEART
CONTINUE TO BE FULL OF
GRACE AND MERCY.

♡ YOUR WIFE

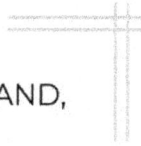

SWEET HUSBAND,

YOU ARE AMAZING. YOU IMPRESS ME
IN ALL THE WAYS.

WE ARE UNDER GRACE, IN THE MOST
PERFECT WAY.

♡ YOUR WIFE

GET TO
KNOW THY SELF

○ _____

○ _____

○ _____

○ _____

○

dear husband,

love,

your wife

1. Appreciation

2. Consideration

3. Goodness

WHAT'S GOOD?

DEAR
HUSBAND,

YOU ARE MY
HERO.

♡ YOUR
WIFE

DEAR
WONDERFUL
HUSBAND,

THANK YOU.

YOU MAKE US
FEEL SAFE,
EVERYDAY.

♡ YOUR
DEVOTED WIFE

Feels Like Fun®

$\mathcal{W}eek$

MONDAY

TUESDAY

WEDNESDAY

THURSDAY

FRIDAY

SATURDAY

SUNDAY

Abundance

SATISFACTION

_____
_____
_____
_____

HEALTHY

WHAT'S GOOD

_____
_____
_____
_____

DEAR
HUSBAND,

I WORSHIP
AND PRAISE

_____
FOR THE WISE
AND KIND
HUSBAND
THAT I HAVE
BEEN GIVEN.

I LOVE TO
CHERISH YOU.

♡ YOUR WIFE

TO MY
HUSBAND,

YOU ALWAYS
MAKE ME
FEEL SPECIAL.

YOU ARE AN
AMAZING
LOVER &
PROVIDER.

♡ YOUR WIFE

DEAR HUSBAND,

I LIKE LEARNING
NEW THINGS WITH
YOU EVERYDAY.

WE ARE BLESSED,
UNDER GRACE, AND
IN THE MOST
PERFECT WAY.

♡ YOUR WIFE

LOVER,

YOU CALM, COMFORT AND EXCITE ME.

 ♡ YOUR WIFE

Communication

DECODE

_____
_____
_____
_____

ENCODE

_____
_____
_____
_____
_____

MEDIA

_____

NOISE

_____

⭐ ⭐ ⭐ ⭐ ⭐

1. Appreciation

2. Consideration

3. Faithfulness

THE BEST THING

DEAR
HUSBAND,

THANK YOU
FOR
LETTING ME
TELL YOU
ABOUT MY
DREAMS.

YOU ARE
THE MOST
BEAUTIFUL
MAN THAT I
HAVE EVER
KNOWN.

PEOPLE

 ♡ YOUR
WIFE

Currency

INCOME

- ♡ _____
- ♡ _____
- ♡ _____

EXPENSES

- ♡ _____
- ♡ _____
- ♡ _____

BUDGETS

- ♡ _____
- ♡ _____
- ♡ _____

21 14 1
16 30 02 28 08 10 21
09 30 12 14 11 06 29
18 07 20 26 03 19 24
25 11 05 04 29 03

M

T

W

T

F

MY
LOVE,

YOU
INSPIRE
ME.

S

♡ YOUR
WIFE

S

MY
HUSBAND,

I LIKE
LEARNING
MORE
ABOUT
HOW TO
BE A
PLEASURE
FOR YOU.

♡ YOUR
WIFE

SWEET
HUSBAND,

YOUR
PATIENCE
AND
WISDOM
GUIDE US TO
NEW AND
HAPPIER
PLACES
EVERYDAY.

♡ YOUR
WIFE

Saying Sweet Things

HELLO HUSBAND,

I LOVE YOUR

_____.

♡ YOUR WIFE

1. Appreciation

2. Consideration

3. Gentleness

Today

MY LOVE,

EVERYDAY IS
A NEW
ADVENTURE
IN TRUST
AND HOPE
AND FAITH
AND LOVE
WITH YOU.

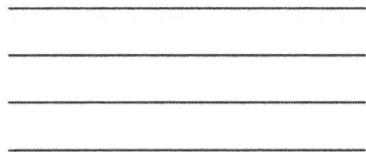

I LIKE IT.

♡ YOUR
WIFE

GOOD

_____
_____
_____
_____

MY HUSBAND,

THANK YOU FOR TAKING
GOOD CARE OF
YOURSELF.

I AM YOUR TEAMMATE.

♡ YOUR WIFE

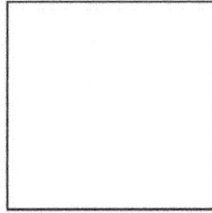

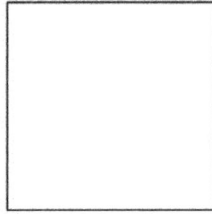

DATA

grateful _____ Date: _____

_____
_____
_____

grateful _____ Date: _____

_____
_____
_____

grateful _____ Date: _____

_____
_____
_____

MY HUSBAND,

THANK YOU FOR
LISTENING TO ME
AND FOR CARING
ABOUT MY
FEELINGS.

♡ YOUR WIFE

_____

_____

_____

_____

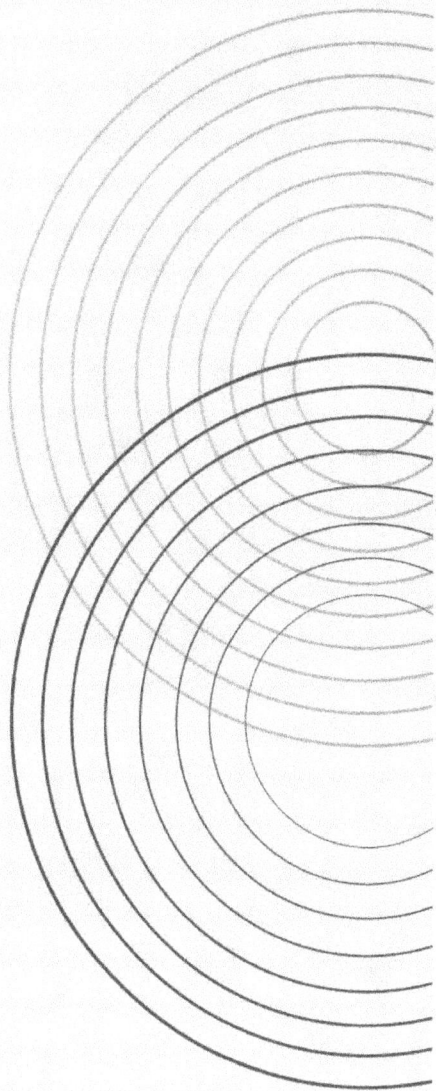

MY HUSBAND,
YOU ARE A GOOD MAN AND I AM IN AWE OF YOU
MORE, EVERY DAY.
♡ YOUR WIFE

1. Appreciation

2. Consideration

3. Self-Control

People

_____
_____
_____

Places

_____
_____
_____

Things

_____
_____
_____

Appreciating

FEELINGS

- _____
- _____
- _____

DEAR HUSBAND,

THANK YOU FOR LOVING
UNCONDITIONALLY.

I LOVE BEING YOURS.

♡ YOUR WIFE

I PREFER

☆ ☆ ☆ ☆ ☆

DEAR HUSBAND,

THANK YOU FOR BEING SO VERY
RESPONSIBLE AND DILIGENT. I LOVE
TO FOLLOW YOUR GRACE AND
AUTHORITY, IN THE MOST PERFECT
WAY.

 ♡ YOUR WIFE

Date:
_____
_____
_____
_____

Date:
_____
_____
_____
_____

Date:
_____
_____
_____
_____

DEAR HUSBAND,

I LIKE TO LEARN
HOW TO BRING YOU
MORE JOY.

♡ YOUR WIFE

My husband is

MY HUSBAND,

THANK YOU FOR LISTENING TO ME AND FOR CARING ABOUT MY FEELINGS.

♡ YOUR WIFE

_____
_____
_____
_____
_____
_____
_____

INSPIRED

DEAR HUSBAND,

I APPRECIATE YOUR DEVOTION AND
COMMITMENT TO TAKING CARE OF MY
LOVE.

♡ YOUR WIFE

Checking in

I AM WORTHY

I AM GOOD

_____
_____
_____
_____

I AM CAPABLE

I AM SATISFIED

I AM FREE
_____

I AM

_____
_____
_____
_____

Rest

dear husband,

♡ your wife